Indians of the Amazon

There were probably around four million Amazon Indians before the arrival of Europeans at the beginning of the sixteenth century. In the succeeding years, the Indian population has been decimated by aggressive Portuguese settlers, epidemics of imported diseases, greedy rubber barons and, more recently, by land-grabbing speculators seeking to make the most of the Amazon basin's mineral wealth, timber and rich pastureland. Today, there are fewer than 100,000 Indians, whose futures have become a very emotional issue. Should they be left to live as they have for thousands of years or be integrated into modern society? The latter option now seems inevitable, and hopefully it can be done without any further bloodshed. Marion Morrison has spent the last twenty years traveling all over the South American continent, frequently to very remote areas, while researching, writing and photographing. She has also written *Indians of the Andes* for this series.

Original Peoples

INDIANS
OF THE AMAZON

Marion Morrison

Rourke Publications, Inc.
Vero Beach, FL 32964

Original Peoples

Eskimos — The Inuit of the Arctic
Maoris of New Zealand
Aborigines of Australia
Plains Indians of North America
South Pacific Islanders
Indians of the Andes
Indians of the Amazon
Bushmen of the Kalahari
Pygmies of Central Africa
Bedouin — The Nomads of the Desert
The Zulus of Southern Africa

Frontispiece *A Yagua Indian man resting in his hammock.*

Text © 1989 Rourke Publications, Inc.

Library of Congress Cataloging-in-Publication Data

Morrison, Marion.
    Indians of the Amazon / Marion Morrison.
        p.   cm.—(Original peoples)
    Reprint. Originally published: Hove, East Sussex,
England : Wayland, 1985.
    Bibliography: p.
    Includes index
    Summary: Introduces the history, culture, and daily
life of the South American Indians who live along the
Amazon basin.
    ISBN 0–86625–266–5
    1. Indians of South America — Amazon River Valley
— Juvenile literature. [1. Indians of South America —
Amazon River Valley. 2. Amazon River Valley.]
I. Title.   II. Series.
[F2519.1.A6M63 1989]
981′.1300498–dc19   88–15073
                                                        CIP
                                                        AC

Manufactured in Italy

Contents

Introduction

The Amazon of South America is the world's greatest river. Everything about it is vast. Rising in the snow-capped Andes 17,000 feet (5,200 meters) above sea level, and just 120 miles (193 km) from the Pacific coast, it flows east for 4,000 miles (6,400 km) across the continent to the Atlantic Ocean. Such is its force that the fresh water penetrates the ocean 150 miles (240 km) out to sea, a fact first noticed by the Spanish sailor Vincente Pinzon, who discovered the Amazon in 1500, and named it "Fresh Water Sea."

The mouth of the Amazon is over 200 miles (320 km) wide. With over 1,100 tributaries, the waters of the great river are said to make up 20 percent of the world's fresh water and drain an area almost the size of the United States. It is a region of tropical rain forest. There are huge trees with tangled lianas and large buttress roots, unfamiliar animals such as the tapir and capybara, and a multitude of colorful birds and insects. Most of the rain forest lies in Brazil, but it extends into eight of its neighboring countries.

In 1541 Francisco Orellana, a Spanish soldier, led the first expedition down the Amazon. The journey took eighteen months and the men encountered many hazards on the way – rapids, starvation and hostile Indians. Legend has it that they came across a tribe of women warriors, the Amazons. It is from these people that the river gets is name.

Beyond the river, in the dark forest, lived many more tribes of Indians who would encounter white men when Portuguese and Spanish colonists began to explore the interior. It was a tragic encounter for the Indians, whose numbers have since been reduced to a fraction of what they were at the time of the European conquest.

Left *A tributary of the Amazon slices through the thick tropical rain forest.*

VENEZUELA

GUYANA

SURINAM

FRENCH GUIANA

COLOMBIA

Makuna
Cubeo

Atroari

Island of Marajo

Manaus

Amazon R.

Omagua

Mura

Xingu R.

Kayapo

Purus R.

BRAZIL

Shipibo

PERU

Cintas Largas

Xingu
National
Park

Txukarramai

Caraja
Kreen-Akrore

Waura

Brasilia

BOLIVIA

Xavante

Yuracare

CHILE

PARAGUAY

ARGENTINA

Rio de Janeiro

Above *This map of South America shows the location of the tribes of Amazon Indians mentioned in this book.*

Left *The capybara is the largest rodent, one of the many unfamiliar animals to be found in the Amazon basin.*

7

Chapter 1 Discovery of the Indians

Origins and legends

Early people arrived in North America from Asia during the Ice Age, crossing the Bering Strait between Siberia and Alaska. They probably accompanied the migration of animals seeking new pastures and a warmer climate. Making their way south some 10,000 to 20,000 years ago, they settled in the forests of South America.

Archaeology in the Amazon basin is difficult. Sites and artifacts are not easily found or preserved because of frequent rainstorms, a very humid climate and fast-growing vegetation.

Also, the early forest-dwellers were nomadic hunters who moved from one place to another in search of game. They built temporary shelters of wood and thatch, materials that quickly decay under such conditions.

The most significant finds have been large natural mounds formed by the accumulation of shells, which were used as burial places. They contain human remains, some crude stone hammers as well as fragments of pottery. These mounds are

Armadillos like this one are part of the Amazon Indian's diet. They are baked in their shells.

Like the early inhabitants of the Amazon's forest, many tribes are still nomadic hunters.

particularly evident on the Island of Marajo, an island the size of Switzerland that lies in the Amazon's mouth. Marajoara pottery is very fine and includes jars, bowls and figurines. From such scant evidence, archaeologists believe people were living in the Amazon basin in 3000 B.C. They have classified four main language groups – Je, Carib, Arawak and Tupi.

There are many Indian legends and myths that tell of their origins. These legends describe gods, jaguars behaving like men, fire devastating the earth, and twins – one good and one bad. Such stories, elaborated over time, are passed from father to son, generation after generation, around the evening family fire.

Time of conquest

The Portuguese Admiral, Pero Alvares Cabral, with a fleet of thirteen ships first sighted the coast of Brazil in April 1500. He was lucky in two ways. First, he had been blown off course while on his way to India, and second, the land he had discovered could be claimed by his king. Following the discovery of America by Columbus in 1492, the Treaty of Tordesillas was signed in 1494. This divided the unknown world between Spain and Portugal. The coast of Brazil fell within the

Admiral Cabral claims Brazil for Portugal on April 22, 1500.

sphere of Portugal.

Cabral stayed only nine days on this visit. He was accompanied by the chronicler Caminha who described their first meeting with the natives: "They were dark and entirely naked, with nothing to cover their private parts, and carried bows and arrows in their hands."

The Indians were expert hunters and fishermen. Using long bows of hard, dark wood and feathered arrows, they could kill with astonishing accuracy. They had no domestic animals and farmed only a few plants, like manioc and maize – a diet that they supplemented with

The Indians have always been expert marksmen with the bow and arrow.

wild honey, nuts, fruits and some edible grubs from the forest.

At first the Portuguese were delighted with the friendly attitude of the natives, but they soon became aware of the aggressive Tupi Indians, who were constantly at war with the other tribes. The fighting and surprise attacks were often very cruel and dominated the native life on the coast. In time, the Portuguese were to learn that colonizing their new territory would not be as simple as it first seemed.

11

Chapter 2 **Disasters of colonization**

Barter to slavery

At first sight, there were no obvious riches in the new territory – no gold, silver or precious minerals. Instead the Portuguese were content to trade the magnificent great tree, the brazil wood, from which they extracted a red dye that was then fashionable in Europe. The tree later gave its name to the country of Brazil.

In return for helping cut and load the giant logs, the Indians were delighted to receive their first metal axes and tools, as well as mirrors, combs and clothing.

Inevitably the coastal supply of brazil wood began to decline, so too did the Indians' interest in their newly acquired gifts. When larger groups of settlers began to arrive on the 2,500-mile (4,000-km) long

Few Indians willingly went to work on the European settlers' sugar plantations, as this picture of a slave army shows.

coast, they looked for a new industry. They found the mild climate ideal for growing sugar. But cutting cane, running mills and boiling molasses involved hard labor that required a large body of men. The Indians, disinterested in acquiring more goods for which they had little use, were unwilling to cooperate – particularly in work that did not require their hunting skills.

The natives quickly became disenchanted with the Europeans. Not only did they resent slavery but also the fact that their women were being taken by the settlers, who clearly had come to stay. In the years that followed, the coastal communities suffered constant war as Indians resisted settlers. Indian fought Indian, and settlers defended the lands they had acquired. Some settlers made huge profits. Thousands of Indians died, while many fled from the coast to seek refuge in the huge Amazon forest.

Sugarcane being harvested on a Brazilian plantation in the seventeenth century.

Plagues from Europe

At the time of discovery, it was generally reported that the Indians were in excellent health, living to a remarkable old age. Not only were there large populations of them living along the Atlantic coast but, as Francisco Orellana observed on his Amazon journey, there also were many large villages along the river. "The further we went, the more thickly populated and better did we find the land," he wrote.

Although the Indians seemed healthy enough, it quickly became apparent that they had no immunity to disease. After the European conquest, widespread epidemics of fever, dysentery, influenza, measles, plague and smallpox took hundreds of thousands of lives. Entire communities and whole tribes of Indians were wiped out.

One group of missionaries did what they could to help the Indians. They were the Jesuits who had been sent to Brazil to convert the natives to Christianity. They set up large mission settlements to which thousands of Indians flocked, both for religious teaching and for protection from the coastal wars. The Jesuits offered the Indians some hope because they opposed slavery. But when the epidemics struck, despite incredible medical efforts by some missionaries, disease spread rapidly through Indian communities.

During the three hundred years of colonial rule, the Indians were the victims of the settlers' fight to survive and to profit, of the Church's desire to convert them to Christianity and of devastating disease.

Brazil became an independent

The Indians gained little from 300 years of Portuguese rule. Even if they survived imported diseases, harsh treatment at the hands of their conquerors resulted in the death of many. And this was before rubber was discovered in the Amazon basin.

A view of Rio de Janeiro, the capital of Brazil until 1960. Discovered in 1502, the Portuguese were responsible for laying the foundations of this thriving port and industrial center.

country in 1822 and slavery was officially abolished in 1888. But this did not protect the Indians when the white man discovered rubber in the upper Amazon.

This seventeenth-century figure of Christ was carved in wood by Guarani Indians under the instruction of Jesuit missionaries. Besides trying to convert the Indians to Christianity, the Jesuits tried to improve the living conditions of the Indians under foreign rule.

Chapter 3 **Way of life**

Harvesting the Amazon

Forest Indians live by a combination of hunting, fishing, gathering wild produce and slash-and-burn agriculture. The Indians cut down trees and burn a clearing to form their field, or "garden," for growing crops. Because Amazon soil is easily exhausted – heavy rains soon wash the nutrients away – the gardens have a short life, and the Indians move on every five years or so.

The Indians' staple crop is manioc, which in its natural state contains poisonous prussic acid. To remove it, the Indians use a *tipiti*, which is a cylindrical press made of vine. Washed manioc is put in the *tipiti* and squeezed to release the poison. The pulp is then dried, mixed into a paste with water and pressed into flat pancake-like loaves. Other cultivated crops include maize, yams,

Txicao women (members of a tribe from the Xingu River region) harvesting manioc.

Txicao boys cut up a tapir that they hunted and killed.

peanuts and bananas. From the forest, Indians gather many other plants, fruits, berries, wild honey and spices, including peppers.

The Amazon teems with fish of all kinds. Even the piranha, or cannibal fish, is good to eat. Some fish, like the *pirarucu*, grow to over 8 feet (2.5 meters) long; while catfish can weigh over 400 lbs (180 kilograms). Indians near rivers never go hungry; they use a variety of bows, arrows, nets, traps and even poisons to catch fish.

Blowpipes are the traditional and most important weapon used by Indians for hunting. A small dart shot from a blowpipe can hit a target some 120 feet (36 meters) away. Sometimes the darts are tipped with curare, a poison that immobilizes climbing animals, causing them to relax their grip and fall to the ground.

Fresh meat also comes from a variety of animals caught in traps and snares or killed with spears and arrows. Wild pigs, rodents of all kinds and tapirs form part of the rich larder provided by the forest.

A well-stocked storehouse

The Amazon Indians have never discovered metal, and in much of the enormous low-lying basin, stone is rare. Despite the lack of these materials, the Indians have perfected substitutes from the natural resources around them.

Arrows and spears, instead of

Men making traps to catch fish.

being tipped with metal, are carved with barbs or points made of immensely hard wood such as that from the *chonta* palm. The same wood is used for making nails to hold pieces of timber together. Alternatively, in places where such hard woods are scarce, the tribes use the bark of trees cut into strips to serve as thongs for binding.

Although they have little need for clothing, most Amazon tribes are expert weavers. Cotton (both wild and cultivated) is woven on looms into hammocks, slings and waist-bands. In some communities in the Andean foothills, long poncho-like garments called *cushmas* are made from cotton. Cloth made from the bark of trees, stamped with painted designs, is used among the Yuracare Indians. Other tribes weave strips of bark and wood into baskets or bowls. These may be waterproofed with gums from a variety of trees.

Fire is known over most of the Amazon basin. Food is baked, grilled or roasted. In places where there is good clay, pottery has been developed. Tribes like the Waura are renowned for their imaginative designs. Otherwise, tribes make use of a variety of containers from turtle shells to vegetable gourds for cooking. Animals such as armadillos can be baked in their shells.

For transportation, the Indians have a variety of craft – rafts made of very light balsawood, dugout canoes and canoes made of bark.

An Indian family enjoying a forest barbecue.

A forest home

Amazon Indian houses are traditionally simple, yet functional, and always built in harmony with the surrounding tropical forest. Made from wood and thatch, these dwellings reflect the nomadic lifestyle of the Indians and are easily discarded when the tribes move on to new locations.

Designs and styles of houses relate to the needs of the people and to their environments. For example, the Caraja have rows of houses along the high banks of the Araguaia River, and the Mura of the Madeira and Purus rivers use canoes, which they convert into dwellings.

Housing also mirrors the economic organization and social structure of the families or village. Sometimes a village may consist of several hundred individuals, but generally, they are small, containing about fifty residents. A characteristic arrangement is seen among the Kayapo Indians of central Brazil. Their houses are arranged around a square, behind which there are huts where the women do the cooking. In the middle of the square is one hut for the men, which can also be used

Over 6½ feet (2 meters) long, the arapaima is one of the largest fish in the Amazon River and its tributaries.

for ceremonial activities.

A feature of the northwest Amazon is the *maloca*. This is a huge communal building, which can accommodate up to two hundred people. Inside there are no walls, but space is allotted to each family. The construction of a *maloca* is very precise: each part has a symbolic meaning. Among the Makuna Indians, for example, the four central posts represent the mountains

An aerial view of a typical Indian village. Made from wood and thatch, its houses are simple but functional.

that support the heavens; the ridge at the top marks the limit of the universe; and the circular floor, the earth. There is little furniture, the Indians sleep on mats or on platform beds, though hammocks are now found all over the Amazon.

Tribal society

Inside Indian houses each family has its own fireplace where everyone gets together to eat or discuss the day's events. Families are large by Western standards, often taking in distant relatives. A happy family unit is fundamental to Indian life and essential for survival. Members of the family are very dependent on each other and content to be so.

Men and women have their allotted tasks. While men clear and prepare gardens, women do the planting and harvesting. Women cook inside the hut, but "forest meals" are prepared by the men. Men never carry water – that is women's work, even on long marches through the forest.

In this relaxed atmosphere children grow up surrounded by love and the attention of all the family. They learn the skills of their tribes not by instruction, but by watching and imitating.

Puberty, or coming-of-age, is an important event in tribal life and celebrated with elaborate festivities. For the children it can be a painful process. Boys are sometimes whipped or subjected to the stings of hornets or poisonous ants. Girls sometimes have their hair shaved or pulled out (the new growth symbolizing the emergence of an adult personality), and often they are kept apart from the rest of the tribe, secluded in a hut for several months. The children undergo these initiation ceremonies without complaint or fear because they accept adulthood and early marriage as part of their responsibilities toward their tribe.

A happy family unit is essential for survival in the tropical forest.

Children learn the skills of their tribes by watching and imitating.

Chapter 4 **A mysterious world**

Indian art

Ceremonial and magical practices play an important part in the life of an Amazon Indian. There are festivals related to the sun, the moon, the seasons, the fertility of plants, birth and, especially, death. All symbolize the Indian belief in

Men playing sacred flutes.

Chief Raoni of the Txukarramai Indians.

spirits and the supernatural, as seen around them in the forest.

At times of festivals, men and women work hard to make their bodies beautiful. Indians love to paint themselves – some because they otherwise feel naked; young men and women to make themselves attractive to the opposite sex; mothers paint babies to put them to sleep. Applying the paint, made from natural dyes, is a group activity and part of the fun of dressing up.

For special occasions, everyone indulges in elaborate adornments. Almost all the ornaments come from nature: necklaces, ear-plugs and nose-pieces of shell, bones and animals' teeth; exquisite multi-colored bands and crowns of feathers made from macaws, parrots and toucans, sweet-smelling tree saps and pungent fruit oils. One tribe, the Cubeo, is famous for its bark-cloth masks representing spirits and

Indians love to decorate themselves.

Bird feathers make a splendid hat.

demons. They are worn to ward off evil powers at funeral ceremonies.

Amazon Indians play pan pipes and flutes made from animal bones or bamboo, drums from animal skins, maracas carved out of gourds, and rattles of nutshells. One special flute is used by some tribes in the Xingu River region. It is nearly 4 feet (1.2 meters) long, made of wood, and emits a deep booming noise like a horn. This flute is believed to be the symbol and voice of a spirit, and must never be seen by women.

27

Jungle magic

Jungle Indians believe spirits control many aspects of their lives, such as good health and a good harvest. They must take care to keep peace with these spirits, which they do through the *shaman*. Any man in a tribe can become a *shaman* if he feels a call to do so and if he is prepared to undergo certain rigorous and frightening ceremonies.

The *shaman* is important to the tribe. He may use his powers to avert storms, to bring success in hunting or to ward off hostile spirits sent by other tribes. He can send out his own spirits to cause damage and disaster to enemies. His social duty is to cure the sick, and he must employ the right spirit to help him. The "fish spirit" may be called upon to spray

A dance to celebrate a successful manioc harvest.

Left *A shaman from the Yagua tribe.*

because of their controlled use, it has been observed that Indians do not seem to suffer ill effects.

Once the drug begins to take effect, the *shaman* chants and dances. He appears to be in another world. He waves his arms in the air and stamps his feet. His postures reflect the personality of the spirit he has chosen to help him. As the effects of the drug wear off, he stops, exhausted, and returns to the normal world in an instant as if nothing has happened.

Below *Quinine bark, which is used by the Indians to cure malaria, eye infections and upset stomachs.*

water over a patient to lower his temperature, while the spirits of monkeys, said to have sticky hands, are used to extract disease from a patient's body.

To assist him in his work, the *shaman* uses special medicinal plants from the forest. Leaves from the jacaranda tree are applied to snakebite, while quinine, from the cinchona tree, is used against malaria, eye infections and upset stomachs. Some native drugs that produce hallucinations, or visions, can be used only by the *shaman*. The *shaman* practices several times each week with these special drugs, and

Chapter 5

Into the twentieth century

Amazon under threat

"Die if need be, never kill." This was the slogan of the great Brazilian explorer Rondon, himself part-Indian. He headed the Indian Protection Service (SPI), which was set up in Brazil in 1910 in the wake of the atrocities of the Rubber Boom.

The problems facing the SPI were immense. Amazon Indians still occupied vast, unknown territories. Some, who had made contact with

Busy, bustling Manaus, once the rubber capital of the world.

whites, had acquired rifles to defend themselves. The so-called Indian problem soon developed into a straightforward dispute over land when the significance of the Amazon basin was appreciated as a source of mineral wealth, oil, valuable wood and lush pasture.

The right of the Indians to the land on which they live, though supported by laws going back to colonial times, has never been enforceable in practice. As a result, and ignoring the Indian presence, vast areas of land were sold to speculators in Brazil, Europe and America. In turn, the development of the land was only achieved at the expense of the Indian. Thousands of them were systematically exterminated by well-armed expeditions. There even were instances of distribution of poisoned food, clothing infected with a smallpox virus, and at least one incident in which Indian villages were bombed from the air. Once an area was cleared of Indians, huge farming combines, landless settlers and gold prospectors took over.

Much of this was carried out with the agreement and knowledge of SPI workers. In 1968 the organization was disbanded in the middle of a great scandal. It was replaced by the National Indian Foundation (FUNAI).

Nothing stands in the way of the Amazon highway as it cuts through the forest.

Xingu: an Indian reservation

In the early 1940s, Orlando Villas Boas and his brothers, Claudio and Leonardo, were in the central Amazon on a government mission to open up land for development. They soon realized that their work, however well-intentioned, meant disaster for the many Indians they met, and they decided to do something about it.

The brothers planned a reservation where the Indians would be encouraged to work and live as they always had, without having to make

Above *Claudio Villas Boas helped set up the Xingu National Park.*

Below *Body-painting is an essential part of daily life for this Xingu woman.*

Room for one more? A Txicao village moving to the Xingu National Park.

a hurried choice between their culture and that of modern Brazil.

In 1961, with the help of FUNAI, the brothers created a national park. The area chosen was around the Xingu River, a region poor in mineral wealth, relatively difficult to get to and to which several tribes had already retreated in the face of the white man's invasions.

Today nearly 2,000 members of fourteen tribal socieities live in the park. They come from several different racial origins and each tribe still speaks its own language and preserves many of its own myths and characteristics. However, through contact with each other over a long period, the tribes have developed some similar customs. Villages are broadly the same, with communal huts in a circle and gardens of manioc and maize nearby.

Medical posts are run with the help of volunteers, and an airstrip has been built by each village so the sick can be flown to the small hospital. The Indians are vaccinated against smallpox and measles because there have been several epidemics. As a result, the number of Indians in the park has increased.

Xingu: success or failure?

Some years ago, one visitor to the park wrote, "The remarkable thing about the Xingu is that is works." But for how long will it continue to work?

In 1971, the Brazilian government announced its gigantic Trans-Amazonica road-building campaign, designed to open up the interior. Highway BR80, originally planned to go around the north end of the park, was suddenly diverted to run straight through it, completely disrupting the villages of the Txukarramai Indians. There was no apparent reason for this sudden change of plan, and the Villas Boas brothers were not consulted.

After the highway was completed, a vast expanse of land north of the road, originally in the park, was put on sale. Again the Txukarramai Indians were disturbed and they reacted violently by killing a number

Xingu Indian chiefs discuss land problems with representatives from FUNAI.

A wrestling contest in a Xingu village.

of white workers on local *fazendas* (farms). Although a compromise was reached over the land, the incident could prove to be a landmark in the history of the Xingu.

The Villas Boas brothers felt obliged to resign from FUNAI and left the Xingu. (Leonardo died in 1962.) Despite thirty years of dedicated work, they saw their original concept of keeping the Indians in isolation eroded by the tribes' contact with white settlers.

This contact often surfaces in the more harmful aspects of civilization – drink, prostitution and violence. Many Indians now understand that money or trading goods can buy small luxuries such as transistor radios and will try to get work on nearby farms in return for pay. Most important perhaps, is the Indians' realization that in order to survive, they must retain the land the government says is legally theirs. And they have shown that they are prepared to kill to protect this heritage.

Uncontacted tribes

Remarkably, there are still unknown tribes hidden in the Amazon forest. In recent years as highways have penetrated deeper into the forest, there has been an even more urgent need to contact these tribes.

In 1968, FUNAI sent three parties to "pacify" three warlike tribes. One team went to the Atroari in the north. Although virtually the entire party was wiped out, a follow-up expedition made peace. The second group went to the Cintas Largas in the west. They had to wait in the jungle for almost two years. Eventually they persuaded some of the tribe to come out of hiding. The third expedition, under the leadership of the Villas Boas brothers, went in search of the Kreen-Akrore.

One of the first signs that this unknown tribe existed came when a young British scientist was attacked and killed in an area where no Indians were thought to live. Then the long-haired Txukarramai captured a small boy from a tribe they called the "people with short hair," the Kreen-Akrore.

Presents are left to encourage the Kreen-Akrore to come out of hiding in the forest.

The Villas Boas brothers first set out by air to locate Kreen-Akrore houses. Rudely constructed of banana leaves, they are difficult to detect through the dense cover of jungle trees. One village was sighted. Later, after struggling upriver for several months, a second Villas Boas expedition reached the village. It was deserted. As is the custom, gifts of mirrors, knives, steel axes and toys for the children were left hanging on trees. The Kreen-Akrore returned to the village, unseen, and took the gifts. This hide-and-seek procedure was maintained, and after many expeditions and frustrations lasting five years, contact was at last made. The Kreen-Akrore were persuaded to move into the Xingu Park. The story does not have a happy ending, however. One report claims that 66 of the original 140 members of the tribe have died from disease.

First contact with members of the Kreen-Akrore.

Chapter 6 **Today and tomorrow**

Headhunters of the Amazon

The Jivaro Indians live on the border of Peru and Ecuador, where the Amazon lowlands meet the jungle-covered eastern slopes of the Andes mountains. They have long been considered one of the most hostile groups in the Amazon, a reputation based on their practice of shrinking the heads of their enemies. In the old Jivaro culture this custom was bound up with a complicated mythology of the soul. It was seen as a way in which a man could become strong and powerful.

With the dawning of the twentieth century and the opening up of the Amazon, many things have changed. The Jivaro no longer shrink heads. The tribe made contact with white civilization when the area in which it lives became part of a colonization program started by the Ecuadorian government. The region is vast, very rich in resources. Even so, it had remained virtually unexplored for centuries.

The colonization program failed because the highland people who tried to work there could not adjust to the different methods of farming, the very humid climate and the poor soil. They abandoned the experiment, leaving behind a network of roads and landing strips.

Meanwhile, a group of Jivaro, the Shuar, had learned enough to set up their own organization to fight for their rights. They created the *Federacion de Centros Shuar* in 1965. The organization now has a membership of 20,000 and many achievements to its credit, notably

The Jivaro Indians have always been considered a hostile tribe because of their practice of shrinking the heads of their enemies, like this one.

the survey and registration of their tribal lands as collective property and a successful radio school system. This unique school system comprises 100 radio schools relaying bilingual lessons to some 2,000 pupils, including children in very remote areas. The programs are specially designed to blend with the social and cultural background of the Indians.

A Jivaro woman preparing food. Note the metal cooking pots in the background.

Adopting Western ways

Western tourists visiting a Yagua village.

Some groups of Indians have already learned to live with modern ideas, though the extent of this integration depends on the circumstances of the tribe.

In the upper tributaries of the Peruvian Amazon are tribes of Indians who were first contacted by missionaries during colonial times. These were the Indians who then found themselves in the center of the Rubber Boom. Now for the first time, in the twentieth century, they have been faced with making their own decisions on modern civilization.

Some have integrated completely, such as the descendants of the Cocama tribe who now live like rural Peruvians. A generation ago the women still wore traditional dress, but this has been rejected in favor of Western-style clothing. The group now speaks Spanish, lives in towns and appears embarrassed if any reference is made to their Indian background.

Their neighbors, the Shipibo, have reacted differently. While accepting some aspects of Western civilization, they have retained many of their Indian traditions. The women wear traditional skirts of hand-woven cotton, with Western-style blouses. The men have Western clothes but put on the traditional *cushmas* for fiestas. Although nominally Catholic, they celebrate some Indian festivals, in particular puberty rights for young girls. The Shipibo have always been known for highly decorated pottery and cloth, which they still make and sell to tourists. One aspect of their tribal life will probably determine their future. The Shipibo are essentially fishermen and where they live is determined by the availability of fish. As the people in towns and communities consume catches from nearby rivers, the Shipibo are being forced to settle in more remote areas where there are few educational or medical facilities.

Many Indians are rejecting traditional dress for Western-style clothing.

Voice in government

Amazon Indians are upheld as survivors of an ancient culture. However, their position as underdog is frequently taken for granted. Even today, their society and the innocent nature of the Indian is abused. One problem is that without education the Indian may never attain a position of authority in the central governments of South America. People of mixed blood have occasionally achieved recognition as writers or artists, but for a pure Indian, a voice in government is almost unknown.

An exception is Mario Juruna, a Xavante Indian from the Mato Grosso (between the Araguaia River and Das Mortes River) in Brazil. He first gained the attention of government authorities in 1974 when he led his tribe in a campaign against land-owners who were encroaching on tribal territory. Bit by bit and with the gradual changes in the political climate, Mario Juruna found himself nationally famous. He was eventually elected in 1983 to the position of Deputy for the State of Rio de Janeiro as a member of one of the opposition parties.

Juruna has learned Portuguese and with his young wife, Doralice, spends much of his time in Rio de Janeiro. He is a popular figure, respected for his traditional Indian honesty. People stop his car in the street to ask for his autograph. He has adopted Western dress, and takes part in many TV debates and

Indian children being taught at a missionary school.

talk shows.

Being an elected Deputy, Juruna is able to travel extensively and make use of modern communications for his campaigns. But more important, he has a vote in the Brazilian government. And although his is only one voice, he has already been able to rally support for Indian causes – especially land disputes.

Shipibo women selling some of their handiwork.

The future

Estimates of the number of Indians living in Brazil are guess work, at best. The original population has been variously recorded as between 2 and 6 million. Of the 230 tribes in existence at the turn of this century, 87 are said to have disappeared by 1968. Today, with no greater degree of certainty, the total number of Indians could be fewer than 100,000.

That is a very small minority when compared with Brazil's total population of 125 million.

To accommodate so many people, there is an increasing need to open up the interior and develop industries. But with each new highway and the destruction of the surrounding forest, the world of the last few Indians is threatened.

The future of the Indians is a very emotional issue in South America.

An Indian boy being injected against a Western disease.

Huge chunks of the Amazon rain forest are being cleared for housing developments.

Should they be left to live as they have for centuries? Or should they be integrated into modern society? There are people who oppose the Villas Boas brothers' policy of isolation. They argue that the Indians already demand tractors, schools and medical assistance, and that they want to help build their country.

The Villas Boas brothers would reply by asking into what can the Indians be integrated? They believe this integration would mean the Indians would live at the lowest level of society, in the slums of the big cities, their culture and traditions having been completely lost.

What do the Indians feel? This is the most difficult question to answer. To step from a Stone Age culture into the technical age of the twentieth century is a daunting prospect.

But the hope must be that improved medical attention and education will help the Indians cope with the integration that now seems inevitable, and that they seem to want. For the moment, as Claudio Villas Boas has observed, "By saving his life, you do not solve the Indian problem, you just preserve the Indian to have a problem about."

45

Glossary

Artifacts The items of ancient civilizations, found by archaeologists.

Blowpipe A hunting weapon made of hard wood, from which small, poisonous darts are blown.

Brazil wood A tree valued for its red dye.

Capybara The world's largest rodent. It lives in Amazon forests.

Chronicler A person who provides a contemporary account of events.

Hallucination Seeing something that is not there, an illusion.

Immunity Having resistance to disease.

Initiation A beginning. As in initiation ceremonies when young Indian boys and girls begin their adult life.

Integration The mixing together of two races of people.

Jesuits An Order of Catholic priests founded by Ignatius Loyola in 1533.

Latex The sap of the rubber tree.

Malaria A fever caused by the bite of a mosquito.

Missionaries The people sent to another country to convert the natives to Christianity.

Molasses A sweet substance produced in the refining of sugar.

Nomadic A way of life in which people have no fixed home, but move on from one place to another

Quinine A bitter-tasting extract of the *cinchona* tree bark, used to control malaria.

Reservation An area of land that is protected for the exclusive use of native tribes.

Speculator A person who takes a risk by investing in land or other business enterprises.

Tapir The largest land mammal in the Amazon.

Vulcanization The industrial process in which rubber is treated with sulfur at high temperatures to provide a strong and flexible material.

Books to read

The Amazon Rain Forests by C.F. Jordan (Springer-Verlag, 1986).

The Emerald Forest by Robert Holdstock (Zoetrope, 1965).

White Waters and Black by Gordon MacCreagh (University of Chicago Press, 1985).

Jacques Cousteau's Amazon Journey by Jacques Cousteau and Morse Richards (Abrams, 1984).

Human Carrying Capacity of the Brazilian Rain Forest by Philip M. Tearnside (Columbia University Press, 1986).

The Fishes and the Forest: Exploration in Amazonian Natural History by Michael Goulding (University of California Press, 1981).

Developing the Amazon by Emilio F. Moran (Indiana University Press, 1981).

Key Environments: Amazonia by G.T. Prance and T.E. Lovejoy (Pergamon, 1985).

Frontier Expansion in Amazonia by Marianne Schmink and Charles H. Wood (University Presses Florida, 1986).

Glossary of Indian, Spanish and Portuguese words

Chonta (pronounced *chon tar*) A palm that supplies both food and hard woods for bows.

Curare *(coo rah ray)* A deadly poison used on blowpipe darts to immobilize or kill.

Cushma *(coosh marh)* A long hand-woven cotton poncho worn mainly by Amazon tribes living near the Andean foothills.

Fazenda *(fa shen dar)* An estate, farm or ranch in Brazil.

FUNAI *(foon aiy)* The initials for the National Indian Foundation (Brazil).

Genipapo *(gen ee papo)* The black dye or body paint taken from the gum of the *genipa americana* tree.

Jacaranda *(jack ahr an dar)* The leaves of the jacaranda tree are used by Indians to relieve snakebites.

Jivaro *(hee vah ro)* A tribe.

Kreen-Akrore *(kren akror ay)* A tribe.

Maloca *(mal lo ka)* A large Indian hut shared by several families.

Manioc *(man ee ok)* The main root crop of the Amazon people.

Maracas *(ma rak ars)* A form of rattle made from gourds filled with pebbles.

Piranha *(pee ran a)* The so-called cannibal fish much feared in Amazon water.

Pirarucu *(pee ra roo co)* The largest scaled fish in the Amazon.

Shaman *(shah man)* A witchdoctor or medicine man.

Shipibo *(ship ee bo)* A tribe.

Shuar *(shoo ar)* A tribe.

Tanga *(tan gar)* A scanty covering, in ancient times made of ceramic. Today it is a tiny bikini.

Tipiti *(tee pee tee)* A tubular press made of braided vine, for squeezing poison out of manioc.

Txukarramai *(ju cahra mei)* A tribe.

Urucu *(u roo co)* A red dye taken from the seeds of the *bixa orellana* shrub.

Yopo *(yop o)* A drug that stimulates hallucinations, used by shamans.

Picture acknowledgments

The illustrations in this book were supplied by the following: Douglas Botting 38; Camerapix Hutchison Library 18, 26 (lower), 27 (upper), 28, 33, 39, and the following pictures from W. Jesco von Puttkamer's collection 9, 19, 20, 21, 24, 25, 27 (lower), 32 (upper), 35, 36, 37, 41, 44; Goodyear Tire & Rubber Co. 16 (right); Mary Evans Picture Library 10, 12, 14; South American Pictures *cover*, *frontispiece*, 6, 11 (Leimbach), 15 (lower), 16 (left), 23 (Leimbach), 26 (upper/Leimbach), 29 (both), 31, 32, (lower/Leimbach), 34 (Leimbach), 40, 42, 43, 45; Wayland Picture Library 7 (both), 8, 13, 15 (top), 16, 22, 30.

Index